Main Battle Tanks

by Melissa Abramovitz

Consultant:
Ryan Yantis
Major, U.S. Army
U.S. Army Public Affairs

CAPSTONE
HIGH-INTEREST
BOOKS

an imprint of Capstone Press
Mankato, Minnesota

Capstone High-Interest Books are published by Capstone Press
151 Good Counsel Drive, P.O. Box 669, Mankato, Minnesota 56002
http://www.capstone-press.com

Library of Congress Cataloging-in-Publication Data
Abramovitz, Melissa, 1954–
    Main battle tanks/by Melissa Abramovitz.
    p. cm.—(Land and sea)
    Includes bibliographical references (p. 45) and index.
    ISBN 0-7368-0757-8
    1. Tanks (Military science)—Juvenile literature. [1. Tanks (Military science)]
I. Title. II. Series: Land and sea (Mankato, Minn.)
UG446.5 .A26 2001
623.7'4752—dc21   00-009750

Summary: Describes the history, design, weapons, and missions of main
battle tanks.

Editorial Credits
Carrie A. Braulick, editor; James Franklin, cover designer; Timothy Halldin,
    production designer and illustrator; Katy Kudela, photo researcher

Photo Credits
Archive Photos, 20; Imperial War Museum/Archive Photos, 16
FPG International LLC, 32
Index Stock Imagery/Michael Burke, 10
Photri-Microstock, cover, 13, 19, 22, 24, 26, 29, 30, 39, 43; Photri-Microstock/
    Mike Pattisall, 14; Erwin C. Nielsen, 34; Gary Bloomfield, 36
Pictor, 4
Unicorn Stock Photos/Chris Boylan, 9
William B. Folsom, 6

Table of Contents

Chapter One

Main Battle Tanks

Main battle tanks are military vehicles. The U.S. Army uses main battle tanks to fight in wars. These tanks have guns to shoot at enemy tanks, soldiers, and aircraft.

Armored Fighting Vehicles

Main battle tanks are a type of armored fighting vehicle (AFV). Other kinds of AFVs include armored personnel carriers (APCs), mechanized infantry combat vehicles (MICVs), and tracked or wheeled reconnaissance vehicles.

Many of these vehicles look similar to main battle tanks. But each AFV has a different purpose. The Army uses APCs and MICVs to

Main battle tanks are equipped with guns to fight enemy forces.

carry soldiers to battles. It uses reconnaissance vehicles to gather information about enemy forces.

Tank Parts

Tanks have two main parts. These parts are the hull and the turret. The hull is the tank's main body. It includes the engine compartment at the tank's rear. It also includes the driver's compartment at the tank's front.

The turret is on top of the tank's hull. The turret contains the tank's main gun. It also contains ammunition. Tank crewmembers fire ammunition such as shells from the main gun. Fire control systems and seats for the crew also are located on the turret. The turret can rotate in a complete circle.

Crew

A tank's crew usually includes four crewmembers. These people include a tank commander, a driver, a gunner, and a loader. The driver sits in the front of the hull. The other crewmembers are located on the turret.

The tank commander has various duties. This crewmember watches the tank's surroundings and

The driver sits in front of the tank's hull. The other crewmembers ride on the turret.

enemy actions. The commander uses an intercom to tell the driver where to steer the tank. The commander uses radios to communicate with crews in other tanks. The commander also tells the gunner when and where to fire the guns.

The gunner and loader help defend the tank from enemy forces. The gunner operates the guns. The loader fills the guns with ammunition. These crewmembers also help the commander keep track of the surroundings.

Tracked Power System

A tank's tracked power system makes the tank move. It also evens out the tank's weight to prevent the tank from sinking into the ground.

Each tank has two tracks. The tracks are made of several sections of steel and rubber called track blocks. The blocks are connected to make a loop.

The tracks are wrapped around heavy, metal wheels called road wheels. Most tanks have five or six road wheels on each side. The road wheels are connected to a sprocket at the tank's rear. Power from the engine turns the

Tank tracks are wrapped around road wheels.

sprocket. The sprocket then turns the road
wheels. This action makes the tank move.

Most modern tanks have turbine engines.
Some tanks have diesel engines. Turbine engines
are much more powerful than diesel engines.
An engine's power is measured in horsepower.
Tanks with a turbine engine can produce 1,500
horsepower. Diesel tank engines can only
produce about 750 horsepower.

A tank's main gun is its most important weapon.

Armor

Armor protects a tank from enemy weapons. This metal covering is on the tank's hull and turret. Most modern tanks have at least 6 inches (15 centimeters) of armor.

Tanks can have one of three types of armor. These are homogenous armor, face-hardened armor, and laminated armor. Homogenous armor has the same metal hardness at all thicknesses.

Face-hardened armor has a hard outer surface and soft inside layers. Both of these armors are made of steel.

Laminated armor is made of layers of different materials such as aluminum, steel, and ceramic. Many military experts believe that Chobham armor is the best laminated armor. The British Army developed this armor in the 1970s.

Some modern tanks have a group of armor panels placed around weaker parts of the tanks. These panels contain explosives. They explode outward when a weapon hits them. The explosion can help prevent damage from the weapons.

Guns

Main battle tanks have powerful guns. They have one large main gun mounted in the turret. They also have machine guns located beside the main gun.

The gunner controls the main gun's movement. Computers usually measure the main gun's position and keep it aimed at targets while the tank moves.

Modern tanks also have a laser range-finder. The gunner shoots a thin beam of light called a laser at the enemy target. Sensors on the tank then determine how far away the enemy is. The range-finder helps the gunner accurately hit targets with the main gun.

Caliber is the measurement of a gun's diameter. This measurement is the distance from one side of a gun's barrel to the other. Caliber is measured in millimeters (mm). Most modern tanks have main guns with a caliber of 120 mm.

In the past, all main guns had spiral grooves in their barrels called rifling. Rifling made the ammunition spin as it was fired. The spinning motion kept the ammunition on course. Today, most tanks have smooth-bored barrels. These barrels fire ammunition with fins. The fins keep the ammunition on course. Smooth-bored barrels shoot ammunition at faster speeds than barrels with rifling. The ammunition then strikes its target with greater force.

Most tanks have two or three machine guns in the turret. These machine guns have much smaller calibers than the main gun. Modern tanks have machine guns that range from about

Tank crews often work in groups called platoons.

7.62 to 12.7 mm. Tank crewmembers use the machine guns to fire at enemy soldiers, vehicles, and aircraft.

Designed for Combat

Crewmembers in a group of four tanks usually enter battles together. These tank groups are called platoons. The tank crews work together to protect each other as they fight.

Tank crewmembers look through periscopes to view their surroundings.

Main battle tanks are equipped to help crewmembers perform combat duties. Tracks and powerful engines help tanks move quickly and easily. Tank hulls are watertight to protect tanks if they cross streams or shallow rivers. Air stays inside the hull.

Tanks have electronic night vision devices called thermal sights. The sights detect heat given off by objects. Crewmembers use thermal sights to locate enemy weapons, vehicles, and soldiers at night. Thermal sights also help crewmembers see through smoke, dust, and rain.

Tanks have periscopes called vision blocks located around all hatches. The vision blocks have mirrors. The mirrors allow crewmembers to see the tank's surroundings without opening a hatch. The crewmembers can view their surroundings in all directions.

Chapter Two

History

Before armies began using tanks, soldiers fought from long, narrow ditches called trenches. They used barbed wire and guns to keep enemies away. Armies performed less trench warfare as tanks became important battle vehicles. The tanks provided soldiers with more protection than trenches. They also enabled soldiers to travel more quickly.

The Tank's Beginning

In 1914, Ernest Swinton was a lieutenant colonel in the British Army. At the time, Great Britain was involved in World War I (1914–1918). The Allies and the Central Powers fought against each other during this

Armies started using tanks during World War I.

war. By the war's end, the Central Powers included Germany, Bulgaria, Austria-Hungary, and Turkey. The Allies included the United States, Britain, France, Russia, Belgium, and Japan. Swinton wanted to use armored vehicles to cross trench lines. These vehicles would be able to push through mud and knock down barbed wire.

Swinton told British military leaders about his idea. Winston Churchill was interested in Swinton's idea. Churchill was a navy commander. He convinced other British military leaders to build the vehicle.

British military leaders wanted to keep their plans secret. They told the builders that the vehicle would be a water carrier in the desert. The builders began calling it a "tank" because they thought it was a water tank. The British later called this tank the Mark 1. They tested the Mark 1 in January 1916.

The Mark 1 was different from today's tanks in some ways. The Mark 1 did not have a turret. Instead, it carried two guns on each of its sides. The guns were in an armored compartment called a sponson. The tracks ran completely around the tank.

tanks had many mechanical problems. They then developed the Renault tank. The French used this tank throughout the war.

The U.S. Army built its first tank near the end of World War I. This tank was similar to the French Renault tank. They called the new tank the M1917. It carried either a 37 mm or a .30 caliber gun on its turret. It traveled 5 miles (8 kilometers) per hour.

Tanks had many uses in World War I. They sometimes cleared a path to allow soldiers to take over trenches. Tanks also dropped long wire ropes with hooks onto barbed wire fences. The tanks then backed up and pulled the barbed wire away.

World War II

By the time World War II (1939–1945) began, militaries around the world had developed several main battle tanks. These militaries often used their tanks during World War II. This war sometimes is called the "Tank War."

The Allied forces fought against the Axis powers during World War II. The Allied forces

The M4 Sherman was the Army's most famous World War II tank.

included the United States, Great Britain, the Soviet Union, Canada, and France. The Axis powers included Germany, Italy, and Japan.

World War II started after Germany invaded Poland on September 1, 1939. The Germans used tanks, soldiers, and airplanes to take over the country. The tank units advanced quickly. Each tank unit took a different route. The tanks surrounded the Polish soldiers.

German soldiers and airplanes then attacked the Polish soldiers. The Germans called this type of attack a "blitzkreig." This word means "lightning war." The blitzkreig attack worked well for the Germans. The Allied forces also began using this type of attack plan.

The M4 Sherman

The U.S. Army built many tanks during World War II. The most famous U.S. tank was the M4 Sherman. The Army built many models of the M4. Most had 3 inches (7.6 centimeters) of armor. They weighed about 30 tons (27 metric tons) and had a top speed of about 25 miles (40 kilometers) per hour. The original M4s had a 75 mm main gun. The Army installed 76 mm main guns on later models.

The Army used many M4s during battles. It often surrounded the German tanks with M4s to destroy them.

M4s were reliable. They often traveled over rough ground without breaking down. They operated well in many climates.

Chapter Three

Modern Tanks

The Army improved its main battle tanks after World War II. Modern tanks have advanced communication and fire control equipment.

The M48 Patton
The Army designed the M48 Patton in 1952. The Army produced more than 11,000 of these tanks by 1959.

The M48 was divided into a driver's compartment, a turret compartment, and an engine compartment. The driver drove the tank from the driver's compartment. The commander, gunner, and loader sat in the turret compartment. A metal fire shield was between the engine

Modern tanks are equipped with a great deal of communication equipment.

The M60 had a 105 mm main gun.

compartment and the turret compartment to protect crewmembers from fires.

The M48 weighed about 52 tons (47 metric tons). It had a top speed of 30 miles (48 kilometers) per hour. The M48 had a 90 mm main gun. It had one 50 mm machine gun. The Army made several models of the M48. Each model had an improved engine or small weapon differences.

The Army stopped using the M48 in the 1980s. Other countries still use this tank. These countries include Greece, Iran, Israel, South Korea, and Spain.

The M60

The Army developed the M60 in the late 1950s. This tank was similar to the M48. It traveled at the same speed. But the M60 carried a 105 mm main gun and three machine guns. It weighed about 57 tons (52 metric tons).

The Army built several models of the M60. In 1962, it built the M60A1. The M60A1 had a small compartment called a bustle at the rear of the turret. The bustle provided the crew with more space. The M60A2 model had a 152 mm main gun. But many turret problems occurred as the Army tested this tank. The Army then stopped producing the M60A2.

The M60A3 had many improvements over the original M60. The M60A3 had a gun stabilizer on the turret. This equipment keeps the main gun pointed at a target even when the tank moves over bumpy ground. The M60A3 also had a smoke discharge system. This system hid the tank in a blanket of smoke.

The M1 Abrams

Today, the Army uses models of the M1 Abrams. These tanks are the Army's newest and most powerful tanks. The Army built the first M1 in 1978. It was the first tank to have a turbine engine.

The original M1 weighs about 54 tons (49 metric tons). Until the early 1980s, it was the heaviest U.S. tank. But the M1's powerful engine moves the tank quickly. Its top speed is 45 miles (72 kilometers) per hour.

The M1 stands lower than most tanks. It is about 8 feet (2.4 meters) tall. Previous tanks were about 12 feet (3.7 meters) tall. This lower height makes it harder for enemies to hit.

The M1 has laminated armor similar to Chobham armor. Some British tanks also have this armor.

Today, the M1 is the Army's only main battle tank in service.

M1s were successful against Iraqi tanks during the Gulf War.

The M1's guns are similar to those of the M60. It has a 105 mm main gun. The M1 also has two 7.62 mm machine guns and one 12.7 mm machine gun.

M1 Abrams Models

Today, the Army usually uses M1A1 and M1A2 models. The M1A1 is similar to the original M1. But it has a 120 mm main gun.

The Army and Marine Corps used about 2,000 M1A1 tanks in the Gulf War (1991). This war began after Iraq invaded Kuwait. The U.S. military helped force Iraq's military out of Kuwait. M1A1 tanks destroyed all types of Iraq's tanks. The Iraqi military destroyed very few M1A1s. Only 18 of these tanks were taken out of service due to damage.

During the Gulf War, the M1A1's night vision equipment helped crewmembers fight battles during the day. Oil wells that caught fire after being destroyed created thick black smoke. The M1A1 crews used their thermal sights to see through the smoke.

The M1A2 has a separate thermal sight for the tank commander. This sight allows the commander to keep better track of the battlefield at night.

The M1A2 also has an Inter-Vehicle Information System (IVIS). This system allows tanks in the platoon to share information with each other. For example, tanks may share

information about their battlefield positions. The information is displayed on a monitor.

The Army sometimes modifies M1 tanks to perform specific missions. Some M1s have mine plows to dig up land mines. The Army also may modify M1 tanks to carry small bridges. These bridges allow the tanks to cross small rivers. Some tanks are modified so they can tow damaged tanks.

The Army sometimes equips M1s with mine plows.

Turret

Road Wheels

Hull

Main Gun

Sprocket

Track

Chapter Four

Anti-tank Weapons

Anti-tank weapons are designed to destroy enemy tanks by firing ammunition or missiles that go through the tank's armor. These weapons include anti-tank cannons and anti-tank missile systems. Anti-tank cannons are large, powerful guns that fire explosive ammunition. Missile systems have launchers. This equipment supports missiles before they are fired.

There are various ways to fire anti-tank weapons. Soldiers sometimes fire missile systems from the ground. Most anti-tank cannons are mounted on tanks or other AFVs. Aircraft also may have anti-tank cannons.

Tanks are able to shoot various types of ammunition from their guns.

APFSDS

A tank's main gun may fire Armor Piercing Fin Stabilized Discarding Sabot (APFSDS). This ammunition consists of a steel, tungsten, or uranium shell that pierces tank armor. Tungsten and uranium are metals that are harder than steel.

The APFSDS shell is smaller than the main gun's barrel. The shell has a casing called a sabot to make it fit inside the barrel. The sabot is left behind after the gun is fired.

APFSDS ammunition can travel through all types of tank armor. The shell travels at a speed of more than 1 mile (1.6 kilometers) per second. It has a range of 2.5 miles (4 kilometers). Range is the maximum distance ammunition can travel to reach its target.

HEAT Ammunition

A tank's main gun sometimes fires HEAT (High Explosive Anti-Tank) ammunition. HEAT ammunition is in a cone-shaped metal case. The shell explodes as it hits a target. The case then pushes through the target.

A tank's main gun fires many types of anti-tank ammunition.

HEAT ammunition has a range of up to 2 miles (3.2 kilometers). HEAT shells cannot pierce some types of laminated armor.

Gunners sometimes fire a HEAT round called MPAT (Multi-Purpose Anti-Tank) ammunition from the main gun. They often fire MPAT ammunition at helicopters. This ammunition explodes when it comes close to its target. Gunners do not need to directly hit the target with MPAT ammunition.

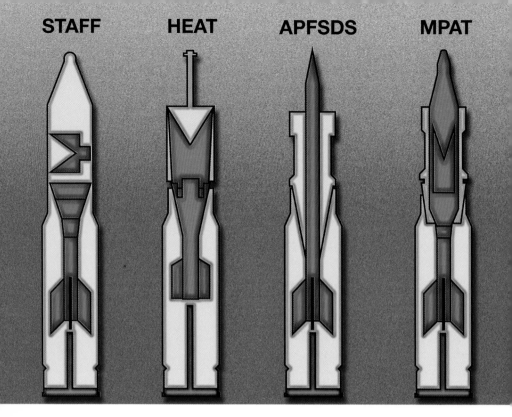

| STAFF | HEAT | APFSDS | MPAT |

STAFF and TERM Ammunition

STAFF (Smart Target Activated Fire and Forget) ammunition is one of the Army's newest shells. The Army developed STAFF in the early 1990s. It plans to equip M1 Abrams tanks with STAFF ammunition. The tank's main gun will fire STAFF shells. These shells have sensors that search for enemy tanks or aircraft. STAFF shells then fire an explosive at the target. They fire the explosive into the top of enemy tanks. This part of tanks is lightly armored.

The Army currently is developing TERM (Tank Extended Range Munition) ammunition. TERM ammunition will allow the M1A2 Abrams' main gun to shoot at targets up to about 5 miles (8 kilometers) away. The M1A2 currently can hit targets up to about 2 miles (3.2 kilometers) away.

TOW Missile System

The Army uses different types of missile systems. It often uses the TOW (Tube Launched Optically Tracked Wire Guided) missile system. AFVs and helicopters can launch TOW missiles. A crew of soldiers also can launch these missiles from the ground.

TOW missiles have a HEAT shell. The shell explodes when the missile hits its target. TOW missiles have a range of about 2 miles (3.2 kilometers).

Other Anti-tank Weapons

Two soldiers on the ground can fire the Javelin missile system at tanks. It has a HEAT shell that explodes when it hits the target. Javelin missiles have a range of about 1 mile (1.6 kilometers)

The AT-4 Anti-tank weapon is the Army's primary light anti-tank weapon. This weapon is lightweight enough for one person to carry it. It weighs 14 pounds (6.4 kilograms). The AT-4 consists of a rocket launcher that fires a HEAT rocket. It has a range of up to 985 feet (300 meters).

The LOSAT (Line of Sight Anti-Tank) missile system launches missiles from a Humvee. These military vehicles are similar to jeeps. The LOSAT system fires missiles at a speed of 5,000 feet (1,524 meters) per second. It has a range of up to 2 miles (3.2 kilometers). LOSAT missiles can travel through all types of armor.

Anti-tank weapons are important to the Army. The Army uses them to destroy many enemy tanks during battles. The Army will continue to improve tank weapons to make tanks even more useful for battles in the future.

The Army plans to equip M1A1s with new weapons in the future.

Words to Know

caliber (cal-UH-bur)—the diameter of the inside of a gun's barrel

horsepower (HORSS-pou-ur)—a unit for measuring an engine's power

periscope (PER-uh-skope)—a vertical tube with mirrors at each end; tank crewmembers use periscopes to view their surroundings in all directions.

platoon (pluh-TOON)—a small group of tanks that work together during battles

range (RAYNJ)—the maximum distance ammunition can travel to reach its target

road wheel (ROHD WEEL)—a large, heavy wheel that connects the track to the tank

sabot (sah-BOH)—a case that protects a shell and fills up the extra space in a gun's barrel

turret (TUR-it)—a rotating structure on top of a tank that contains the tank's main gun

To Learn More

Black, Michael A. *Tanks: The M1A1 Abrams.* High-Tech Military Weapons. New York: Children's Press, 2000.

Green, Michael. *The United States Army.* Serving Your Country. Mankato, Minn.: Capstone High-Interest Books, 1998.

Guy, John. *The History of Weapons And Warfare.* The History Of. Hauppauge, NY: Barron's Educational Series, 1998.

Useful Addresses

U.S. Army Center of Military History
103 Third Avenue
Fort McNair, DC 20319-5058

U.S. Army Public Affairs
Office of the Chief of Public Affairs
1500 Army Pentagon
Washington, DC 20310-1500

Internet Sites

Federation of American Scientists—Military Analysis Network
http://www.fas.org/man/index.html

M1 Abrams Main Battle Tank
http://www.dmi.usma.edu/Intersession/ms302/web/m1a1_pg.htm

Tanks!
http://mailer.fsu.edu/~akirk/tanks

The U.S. Army
http://www.army.mil

Index